TESSA KIROS

A

VENETIAN
JOURNAL

food, travel, dreams

MURDOCH BOOKS

Venezpia

My Beginning

Venice is one of those places you could most probably cartwheel into unnoticed. Once you had landed on your feet, you'd be held fixed for a moment and forced to stare for a while, before stepping your way into this magical place and losing your way through secret passageways and tiny roads uniting with bridges over the water. You'd be forgiven for feeling you were suddenly a member of an impromptu cast as you shuffled along with the crowds. Or if it were carnevale, you'd be pardoned for thinking you had embarked upon another world as you laced your way through the characters.

You would discover some wonderful places, stopping to have an ombra ('a shadow' — one of Veneto's beauties in a glass) at any odd time of day or night. Among Venetian chatter you could reach out for a small bite called cicchetti (chi-ket-tee). Multiple choices just a toothpick away from you. You could make it quick or linger — and this lack of rigidity could just get you into the greatest of good moods.

The end of the day could find you sinking into a chair in one of the many fine campi (Venetian lounges), sipping spritz or bellini, sprinkling your Italian here and there, watching it all happen as you sifted through the things collected.

PERSONAL DETAILS

NAME . . . .

ADDRESS . . . .

TELEPHONE . . . .

BEST FRIEND . . . .

MY HEIGHT . . . .

SIZE OF HAT . . . . COLLAR . . . .

SHIRT SIZE . . . . SLEEVE LENGTH . . . .

GLOVE SIZE . . . .

SHOE SIZE: AMERICAN . . . . EURO . . . . UK . . . .

MAKE OF WATCH . . . .

STAR SIGN . . . .

FAVORITE MEAL . . . .

FAVOURITE SONG . . . .

MEMORABLE SAYING . . . .

. . . .

a di
rgio Maggiore»

I

ESSENTIALS

patterns & prosecco

Masterpieces everywhere you look...

Spritz

Red & orange

4–5 ice cubes
60 ml (2 fl oz/¼ cup) aperol
  or campari
60 ml (2 fl oz/¼ cup) white
  wine or prosecco
60 ml (2 fl oz/¼ cup)
  soda/seltz
a thickish chunk of orange
  with skin
1 olive, shaken out of brine &
  threaded onto a cocktail stick

This is a much appreciated aperitivo in Venice. To make a Spritz, take a large wine glass & add a good splash of an aperitif, such as campari or its lower-alcohol version, aperol. Next comes a good splash of white wine or prosecco & a few ice cubes. A splash of soda water (club soda, or 'seltz' in the bars) is next because it revs everything up from bottom to top, & last, a piece of orange and a green olive on a cocktail stick. The olive is in brine & not rinsed, the lady says. The drink comes halfway to three-quarters up the glass. Very nice.

Everyone has their own way of Spritz. Use aperol or campari or whatever you prefer. Some people say no olive, others no orange. One wants a piece of lemon, one wants prosecco instead of the wine, one no wine at all – it's a bit like how you take your coffee – rather personal. So here's a rough guide to how I like my Spritz.

Adjust yours to suit your personal preferences.

_Put the ice in a large wine glass. Splash in the aperol and then the white wine, next a good whoosh of fizzy water to get everything moving and mixed in. Add the orange and olive on a cocktail stick. That's it.

Serves 1

❧ *Bellini* ❧

cin cin

1 beautiful sweet ripe white peach (about 150 g/5 oz)
a couple of raspberries
240 ml (8 fl oz) cold, cold prosecco, or more if you like

Prosecco has its own kingdom in Venice. Not just any prosecco will do & there is even a separate wine list in some restaurants. Over many lunches I noticed people drinking full rounded plump bottles of chilled prosecco rather than wine, especially with their seafood… beautiful. Never mind stirring it into beautiful puréed white peaches & other fruits. These are the measures I like, but, of course, they're just rough estimates, depending on your glasses and such. They are easy to double or triple for more people, and add more prosecco or fruit, depending on your personal preferences. This is nice served with a raspberry, or you could purée a couple of raspberries and add, for a pinkier colour.

__Peel your peach with a sharp knife (or plunge it briefly into boiling water if the skin won't budge). Halve & stone the peach & purée until smooth. You can sieve your purée or leave it rough — either is good. You can add a little sugar & a drop of lemon if you like once you have tasted your purée (it will depend on your peach).
__Throw in one raspberry per glass. Pour the peach purée into large, beautiful, well-chilled glasses. Stir in the prosecco & wait for it to settle. Serve at once.

Serves 2

Nota bene

Nota bene

II

~Tramezzini~

Italian sandwiches

The tramezzini are classic little sandwiches — white bread, stuffed to bursting with mayonnaise & other fillings — that have been updated by the cicchetti bars of modern Venice. They are an important part of Venetian life & are served often with a lovely glass of wine. You need squares of thin white bread with the crusts cut off (about 10 cm/4 inches square), which you then halve into two triangles. The tramezzini are stuffed in the middle & taper down on the corners. Keep them covered if you won't be serving them immediately, so the edges don't curl up.

These are what we filled ours with:

__a layer of mayonnaise, then a small slice of ham & 2 artichoke quarters (*the ones bottled in oil*);
__a layer of mayonnaise, a tablespoon or so of crumbled drained tuna, 3 opened-out capers & a slice of hard-boiled egg in the middle;
__chopped/puréed blanched asparagus mixed with a little mayonnaise (*about 1 tablespoon mayonnaise to 1 tablespoon asparagus purée*), poached scampi, a couple of blanched asparagus tips & a sprinkling of ground pepper. Add a dab more mayonnaise to keep the top slice of bread in place;
__a layer of tuna salsa (*pulse a tin of drained tuna in oil with 1 large tablespoon capers until smooth-ish, then mix with 3 tablespoons mayonnaise*), some crumbled drained tuna, sliced pickled cucumbers & a dab more *salsa* on the top piece of bread;
__a layer of mayonnaise, sliced egg, artichoke quarters (*the ones bottled in oil*) & ground pepper;
__or any other filling you like.

Sarde in saor

Sardines sour

about 125 ml (4 fl oz/½ cup) olive oil

400 g (14 oz) white onions, halved & thinly sliced

a few whole peppercorns, gently squashed

2 bay leaves

125 ml (4 fl oz/½ cup) white wine vinegar

15–18 whole sardines, about 500 g (1 lb 2 oz)

flour, for dusting

light olive oil, for frying

Every Venetian I have met loves sardines cooked like this — in saor means literally 'in a sour sauce'. My sister-in-law, Luisa, has fond memories of her grandmother often making a big glass bowlful. They make a great snack if you have a crowd to feed — not only because you can easily make many batches, but because they keep so well in the fridge. I think they taste best after at least a couple of days to soak up all the delicious flavours. If you are making a large quantity you may have to wash out the pan & start with a fresh batch of oil if the flour starts to burn. If you want to add extra flavour, do as many Venetians do & add a handful of pine nuts & raisins to the onions. I use smallish sardines — you can leave their tails on or off as you prefer.

__Heat the oil in a non-stick frying pan with a lid, add the onions & cook over medium heat. After a few minutes, add the peppercorns, bay leaves & some salt & pepper, put the lid on, lower the heat & simmer for 20–25 minutes. The onions must not brown but be well softened & nicely cooked, so check from time to time that not all the liquid has been absorbed. If the onions are browning too much, add a few drops of water & carry on simmering. Once the onions are soft & cooked down, add the vinegar & simmer without the lid for another 5–10 minutes until reduced a little, leaving the onions covered in a lovely sauce, but don't let them dry out.

__Meanwhile, to fillet the sardines, cut off the heads, then make a slit down the side of each fish & remove the guts. Open out the sardines like a book so they are still hinged together & place, skin-side up on a chopping board. Press each sardine lightly, yet firmly, to open out. Turn each over & pull out the backbone *(or leave in the bone & just clean them while you are eating them)*. Rinse & pat dry. Pat well in the flour to coat on both sides.

__Pour enough oil into a large non-stick frying pan to cover the bottom abundantly. When the oil is hot add the sardines, turning them only when they are crisp on the bottom. If the flour is falling off the sardines & sticking to the bottom, you may need to reduce the heat a touch. When both sides are golden & quite crisp remove to a plate lined with kitchen paper to absorb the excess oil. Sprinkle with fine salt.

__Layer the sardines & onions in a compact bowl, seasoning as you go, creating about three layers. Add in the squashed peppercorns & a splash more oil if it looks as if it needs it. Cover & either leave at room temperature if you will be eating within the next few hours or put in the fridge where they will keep for a few days. Each time you eat a sardine, rotate the rest so that they are all covered & not just the underneath ones.

Note #1

Bring galoshes to Venice, if you can. Try to find out how the weather will be. Then, if it says rain, bring the galoshes. If not, you can buy them. It's no fun in Venice with rain, lagoons and no galoshes.

Bella Venezia

capolavoro–*masterpiece*–adesso–*now*
bambini–*children*–angeli–*angels*–bellissimo–*beauty*
lucciola–*firefly*–ciao–azzurro–*azure*
ancora–*more*–amore–*love*–sguardo–*glance*

III

ANTIPASTI

pearls & paintings

Acqua frizzante, acqua naturale, acqua alta, acqua acqua...

La saltata di vongole alla marinara

Clams & tomato

Tomato sauce:

4 tablespoons olive oil

½ small onion, very finely chopped

375 g (13 oz/1½ cups) tomato passata

a good pinch of peperoncino

2 tablespoons cream

Clams:

3 tablespoons olive oil

2 garlic cloves, chopped

1 kg (2 lb 4 oz) vongole veraci in shells

125 ml (4 fl oz/½ cup) white wine

This is how my lovely sister-in-law, Luisa (half-Venetian, half-Tuscan), likes to make clams. She adds a dash of cream to the tomato sauce, which makes it beautifully sweet & mellow. These can be served with bread or are great tossed into pasta with a little of the pasta cooking water to loosen things up. Try penne, spaghetti or any pasta you like: you'll need about 280 g (10 oz). You can also add a handful of chopped herbs to the sauce if you like. I have used vongole veraci (carpet shell clams) here but any vongole are fine. Your clams will probably have been purged of sand already but check with the fishmonger, otherwise you'll need to soak them for a day in a colander standing in well-salted water, changing the water several times.

__To make the tomato sauce, heat the oil in a frying pan & cook the onion over low heat until it almost disappears & is very soft (*it should not be dark but should be very well cooked*). Add the passata, a grinding of salt & pepper & a good pinch of peperoncino. Simmer uncovered for 10–15 minutes until it all thickens into a lovely sauce. Add the cream & allow the sauce to bubble for a couple of minutes more. Take the pan off the heat.

__If you've been soaking your clams, give them a good swirl in the water, rinse them, drain & leave in the colander. Heat the oil with the garlic in a large frying pan (*that has a lid*). Once you start to smell the garlic, add the clams & wine. Turn the heat up to the maximum & put the lid on the pan. Let the clams all steam open. Discard any that refuse to open.

__Take the clams out of the pan. Check for sand by pressing on the bottom of the pan with the back of a spoon. If you think there might be sand, then strain the sauce through a colander lined with muslin.

__Add all the clam water to the tomato sauce & simmer for 5–10 minutes until the flavours have merged & the liquid reduced a little. You want there to be quite a lot of liquid but it shouldn't be too watery. Return the clams to the pan & heat through for a minute. Serve straight from the pan with bread.

Serves 4

Carpaccio di carne

Meat carpaccio

1 beautiful artichoke suitable
  for eating raw
125 g (4 oz) very thinly
  sliced beef
juice of half a lemon
table & coarse pounded salt
2 tablespoons extra virgin
  olive oil
about 20 g (1 oz) shaved
  parmesan or asiago stagionato
bread, to serve

Harry's Bar made this famous. The carpaccio there is excellent & is served with a creamy mayonnaise sauce drizzled over. Here I have served it with artichoke & a lemon oil. You could also serve it with rocket, or thin slices of endive, fennel or celeriac. A couple of blobs of a creamy blue cheese here & there also work well. Serve this as an antipasto for two or a secondo for one. It is lovely as a summer lunch with a green salad on the side & some bread, & then it can take something slightly richer for dessert.

Use well trimmed & tender flavoursome lean beef, such as girello, shell steak (use strip loin or porterhouse) or tenderloin (mid loin). Beef fillet works well, too. The diametre of the meat is not important; just add more slices to the plate to cover it, overlapping slightly if necessary. Ask the butcher to trim the meat for you. You may even be able to convince him to slice it, but only if you plan to serve it within an hour or two. If you slice the meat yourself, cut it very cold from the fridge to get the thinnest possible slices. It is important the meat is thin thin & soft soft. Add some coarse pounded salt in too for the texture — table salt with a small amount of bashed coarse salt added.

_Prepare your artichoke first. Trim away the outer leaves & cut a slice off the top. Halve the artichoke & remove the hairy choke if it has one, then cut each half into fine slices 1–2 mm thick. (*If you're not serving immediately, keep them covered with cold water & a little lemon juice to prevent them turning black.*)
_If necessary, put the beef slices between two sheets of plastic wrap & pound with a meat mallet until very thin. Arrange them flat on a large plate, slightly overlapping is fine. Scatter the artichoke slices over the top. Drizzle with lemon juice, sprinkle with the salt & drizzle with oil. Now scatter the cheese on top & a good grind of black pepper. Serve with bread & perhaps the bottle of olive oil, salt & black pepper on the side in case you need extra.

Serves 2

Tuesday..

Wednesday......................................

Thursday..

Friday ....

Saturday...

Sunday...

Monday...

Tuesday..

Wednesday...................................

Thursday.......................................

Friday ....

Saturday.......................................

Sunday...

Monday..

Pasta e fagioli

Pasta & beans

300 g (10½ oz) dried Lamon
  or borlotti beans
1 carrot, peeled
1 celery stalk
2 garlic cloves, peeled but
  left whole
2 onions, peeled, 1 left whole
  & the other finely chopped
4 tablespoons olive oil
150 g (5½ oz) pancetta
  (unsmoked), chopped
a little pinch of peperoncino
1 tablespoon chopped rosemary
125 g (4½ oz) dry pasta, such
  as thin tagliatelle or tagliolini,
  broken up
thin slices of firm, mature asiago
  or pecorino, to serve
a drizzle of olive oil

*This soup is served everywhere in Venice, made with various types of pasta.
I particularly like this version that I ate at Marinella's restaurant, La Buona
Forchetta, which she served with tagliolini that had been broken up & small
triangles of mature asiago. When cooking it at home, you can use any type of short
dry pasta (not fresh pasta). I've also seen it with torn & lightly dressed radicchio
on top. You can make the soup beforehand & keep it in the fridge for a day
(you will need to add water when reheating, though).*
   *Lamon beans are the large creamy speckled beans found in the Veneto region.
They need to be soaked overnight & then cooked for 30–45 minutes until tender.
If you can't source Lamon beans use borlotti beans, which may need longer cooking
& perhaps more water.*

__Put the beans in a large bowl, cover with cold water & leave to soak for
8–10 hours or overnight. Drain & put the beans in a large pot with the
carrot, celery, garlic, the whole onion & 2 litres (70 fl oz/8 cups) of water.
Bring to the boil & skim the surface.

__Lower the heat, partly cover the pot & simmer from 30 minutes to 1 hour
depending on the type & age of your beans & the heat of the stove. You
want the beans to be soft & creamy but not too mushy. You may need to
add 500 ml (17 fl oz/2 cups) of hot water midway through cooking so you
have a good amount of liquid without it being too watery. Season towards
the end of the cooking time with salt.

__While the beans are cooking, put the oil & chopped onion into a wider,
flatter pot & sauté until the onion is softened. Add the pancetta & carry on
sautéing until the onion & pancetta are golden but not too crisp. Add the
peperoncino & some salt & pepper & stir in the rosemary for a minute or
so on the heat then remove the pan from the heat & cover.

__Take the beans off the heat when cooked. Lift out & discard the whole carrot, celery & onion. Lift out an abundant slotted spoonful of the whole beans & put into the pancetta pot. Take 2 tablespoons of the chopped onion & pancetta mixture & put into the bean pot — a fair swap.

__Purée the bean mixture in a blender until completely smooth, then return to the pot, add the pancetta & onion, stir briefly & bring to the boil. Stir in the pasta pieces & cook for a few minutes until tender. If the soup is too thick for your liking, add more hot water.

__Taste to see if you need more salt & pepper. Ladle the soup into bowls & top each bowl with a couple of thin triangles of cheese so they melt a bit. Add a drizzle of oil & a grinding of pepper.

Serves 4–5

Perruquier Barbier, Perruquier

Spaghetti al nero di seppie

Spaghetti with squid ink

300 g (10½ oz) squid, with
  ink sac
3 tablespoons olive oil
2 garlic cloves, chopped
a pinch of peperoncino
1 tablespoon chopped parsley,
  plus some for serving
125 ml (4 fl oz/½ cup) white
  wine
140 g (5 oz) spaghetti

This is an aesthetically dramatic dish — jet black — which is how I like it, but if you prefer a softer look, add less squid ink. If your squid doesn't come with an ink sac or if it doesn't yield much ink, you can use a sachet of squid ink. These are sold by some fishmongers & delicatessens, often in a package containing 2 sachets of 4 g (⅛ oz) per packet. You should only need to use 1 sachet here, but you can add another one if you want the result to be blacker. Alternatively, you can make the sauce without any squid ink at all & mix it with black ready-made squid ink spaghetti.

__To prepare the squid, pull the head & innards from the body. Separate the ink sac from the rest of the innards without puncturing, then rinse gently & put in a bowl. Wash the body. Cut off the head just below the eyes, leaving the tentacles in one piece, & discard the head. Pull out the transparent quill, rinse the tube & peel off the outer membrane. Cut the squid body into 6 mm (¼ inch) strips & the tentacles into pieces. Pat dry with kitchen paper.
__Heat the oil in a non-stick frying pan that has a lid & add the squid. Cook over high heat until the liquid begins to evaporate, then add the garlic, peperoncino & parsley & season with salt & pepper. When you can smell the garlic, add the wine & bring it to a simmer. Once it is bubbling up, cover with the lid, lower the heat & simmer for 10–15 minutes until most of the liquid has been absorbed.
__Cut the ink sac into a cup & mix with 185 ml (6 fl oz/¾ cup) of water. Pour into the pan. Add a little more water to rinse out the inky cup, pouring it into the pan. Cover & simmer for 15 minutes or until the squid is tender (*check it's not drying out & add water if necessary*). Taste for salt.
__Meanwhile, cook the pasta in boiling salted water until tender. Drain, reserving ½ cupful of the cooking water. Add the pasta & cooking water to the pan with the squid & toss well to coat with sauce. Serve with a little extra parsley and a good grind of black pepper, even though you won't see it!

Serves 2

Note #2

Venice is such a prima donna. Whatever tides, acqua alta or other she decides — we all have to follow on... she forces you to sway to her temperament and nature. You must surrender.

V

RISO

patience & plenty

Festina lente

Risi e bisi

Rice & peas

900 g (2 lb) fresh peas, shelled
   or 450 g (1 lb) frozen peas
1.75 litres (59 fl oz/7 cups) hot
   vegetable broth
12 thin slices cured unsmoked
   pancetta/rigatino (the
   peppery, salty one)
3 tablespoons olive oil
1 small white onion, chopped
2 tablespoons chopped parsley,
   plus some for serving
250 g (9 oz) risotto rice
125 ml (4 fl oz/½ cup) white
   wine
1 tablespoon butter
2 tablespoons grated parmesan,
   plus some for serving

This dish was traditionally good enough for the doges. It becomes an altogether different plate if you use shelled home-grown peas, & add the jackets to your broth as it simmers. If you are serving 6 you will want to have 4 more slices of pancetta to crisp up for the top. You could also add a fresh herb in here last minute.

__If you are using fresh peas, shell them & add the pods to your vegetable broth as it cooks.

__Chop 4 slices pancetta, reserving the rest for later. Heat the oil in a wide heavy-based saucepan or deep frying pan. Sauté the onion until golden & cooked through well. Add the chopped pancetta & cook briefly until softened. Add the peas & 1 tablespoon of the parsley & simmer for a minute. Add the rice & stir until it is well coated with the oil. Pour in the wine & let it bubble up for a few minutes to reduce the wine & mingle the flavours.

__When much of the wine has been absorbed, add 500 ml (17 fl oz/2 cups) of hot broth & continue cooking, stirring regularly & adding another 500 ml (17 fl oz/2 cups) more broth as it is absorbed, for about 20 minutes, or until the rice is tender. Check for seasoning. Just before the rice is cooked, add another 1 or 2 cupfuls of the broth & mix to make sure nothing is sticking. Taste for seasoning, but remember that you will be adding parmesan. Add the butter, the remaining tablespoon of chopped parsley & the parmesan & stir through. (*This should be a loose risotto, with some thick liquid running around the side, like a lovely soupy rice.*)

__Meanwhile, heat up a non-stick pan (*you shouldn't need any oil*) & fry the thin slices of pancetta until crisp & golden.

__Serve the risotto with black pepper & a good scattering of parmesan on top. Put a couple of slices of crisp pancetta on top of each serving & sprinkle with more parsley & grated parmesan or pecorino if you like.

Serves 4–6

Risotto di asparagi e scampi

Asparagus & scampi risotto

12–16 scampi (red-claw,
   langoustines) or large prawns

Brodo:
1 large carrot
½ onion
1 bay leaf
a few peppercorns

360 g (13 oz) asparagus
½ onion, finely chopped
4 tablespoons olive oil
250 g (9 oz) risotto rice
125 ml (4 fl oz/½ cup) white
   wine
1 tablespoon cognac
1 tablespoon butter
2 tablespoons grated parmesan

This is also good & delicate with just scampi or just asparagus. Some people don't serve parmesan with seafood, but I put a bit in here.

__To make the brodo, peel & clean the scampi & halve them down the middle. Set the meat aside for now, but rinse the heads & shells & put them in a pot with 1.5 litres (52 fl oz/6 cups) of water, the carrot, onion, bay leaf, peppercorns & some salt. Bring to the boil, then simmer for 30 minutes. Strain & keep the broth hot.

__Discard the woody ends from the asparagus & cut off the tips. Keep the tips on one side & chop the stems. Sauté the onion in 3 tablespoons of the olive oil until well softened, add the chopped asparagus & sauté briefly.

__Add the rice, turning it through so it is well coated with oil. Add the white wine & let it bubble up until much of it has evaporated. Add 500 ml (17 fl oz/2 cups) of broth, stir well & simmer for 10–15 minutes or until it has almost all been absorbed. Add another 2 cupfuls of broth, stir & cook for another 5–10 minutes. Add another ½ cup of broth if you need it for a creamy risotto.

__When your risotto is almost ready, heat the remaining oil in a small pan, add the scampi & asparagus tips & cook over high heat for 2 minutes, turning the scampi over when they have a pale golden crust underneath. Add the cognac, stand back & flame the pan. Add a bit of salt & toss it all together, then take off the heat.

__Stir the butter & parmesan into the risotto, then tip the scampi & asparagus tips into the risotto. Add salt if needed, quickly toss it all through & serve at once with black pepper.

Serves 4

UNA MASCHERA

Cut along the dotted line
Taglia lungo la linea tratteggiata

VI

SECONDI

fritto & friends

Fritto misto di pesce

Mixed fried fish

8 calamari
light olive oil, for frying
8 scampi tails (red-claw,
   langoustines) or large prawns,
   peeled & deveined
2 small whole sole (about
   70 g/2½ oz each) or other
   small fish, cleaned & gutted
flour, for dusting
lemon, to serve, if you like

This is everywhere in Venice, featuring many different seafoods… sometimes with tiny whole baby squid which are much appreciated by the Venetians. Eel is also appreciated, or you could use any fresh fish you like; sometimes vegetable sticks are on the platter, too. This is a combination I like. Generally, the amounts for a fritto in Venice tend to be rather generous, but you can judge for yourself. I prefer to eat this for lunch rather than dinner & just have a salad on the table as well. Many Venetians say you don't need lemon here — they prefer to taste just the freshness of fish. You decide.

__To prepare the calamari, firmly pull the head & innards from the body & wash the body well. Cut off the head just below the eyes, leaving the tentacles in one piece if they're small. Discard the head, pull the transparent quill out of the body & rinse out the tube. Peel off the outer membrane & cut the tube into chunky rings, about 3–4 cm (1½ inches) thick.
__Heat enough oil in a large deep pan or wok to comfortably fry the fish. Pat all the seafood dry with kitchen paper, pat in flour & shake off the excess. Your oil must be HOT HOT before you add anything. Start with the sole (*they will take the longest to cook*) & a few calamari if they fit — once the sole are crisp & golden on both sides (& *cooked on the inside*) lift out with a slotted spoon onto a plate lined with kitchen paper.
__Add all the calamari to the pan, & the scampi too, if they fit. When golden, lift out to drain on more kitchen paper. Move to a dish (*lined with paper for serving, if necessary*).
__Serve with salt & black pepper… lemon for squeezing… cold white wine or prosecco. At once.

Serves 2

Fegato alla Veneziana

Liver & onions

200 g (7 oz) calf liver
1 tablespoon butter
2 tablespoons olive oil
200 g (7 oz) white onion,
    halved & thinly sliced
a couple of sage sprigs
80 ml (2½ fl oz/⅓ cup) white
    wine
1 heaped tablespoon chopped
    parsley
soft or grilled polenta, to serve

This is on every menu in Venice. You can easily double the recipe if you're serving more than a couple. Some people use 2 pans & cook the onions & liver separately, then unite them in one pan shortly before serving. The most important thing here is that the liver is top quality, so when it's cooked it should be very soft. Sergia, a Venetian angel, adds a couple of unpeeled apple slices, too, to make the onions more 'digestible'. While it may not be very traditional, I like the sage in here.

__Wash the liver in cold water, pat dry & cut away any sinew. Slice into 2–3 mm (¹⁄₁₆–⅛ inch) pieces. Then cut more or less into triangles about 7 x 2 cm (2¾ x ¾ inches).

__Melt the butter in a large non-stick frying pan that has a lid, then add the oil. When hot, add the onion & cook, stirring, for a couple of minutes to get them going before adding the sage & a little salt. Cover & simmer over low heat for 15–20 minutes until soft & very pale golden. Add the wine if anything looks like it could be starting to catch or in the last 10 minutes or so. Stir often so nothing sticks.

__Take the lid off, move the onion to the side of the pan (*or remove to a plate*), turn the heat right up & add the liver. Cook for a couple of minutes until cooked through & just starting to change colour, turning halfway so both sides are browned. Once cooked, add salt & pepper (*& return the onion if you took it out of the pan*). Take the pan off the heat add the parsley. Serve at once with soft or grilled polenta.

Serves 2

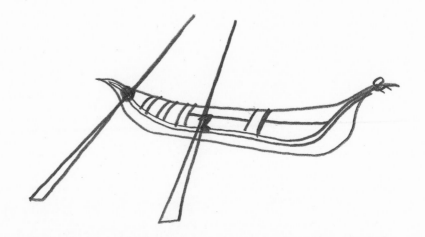

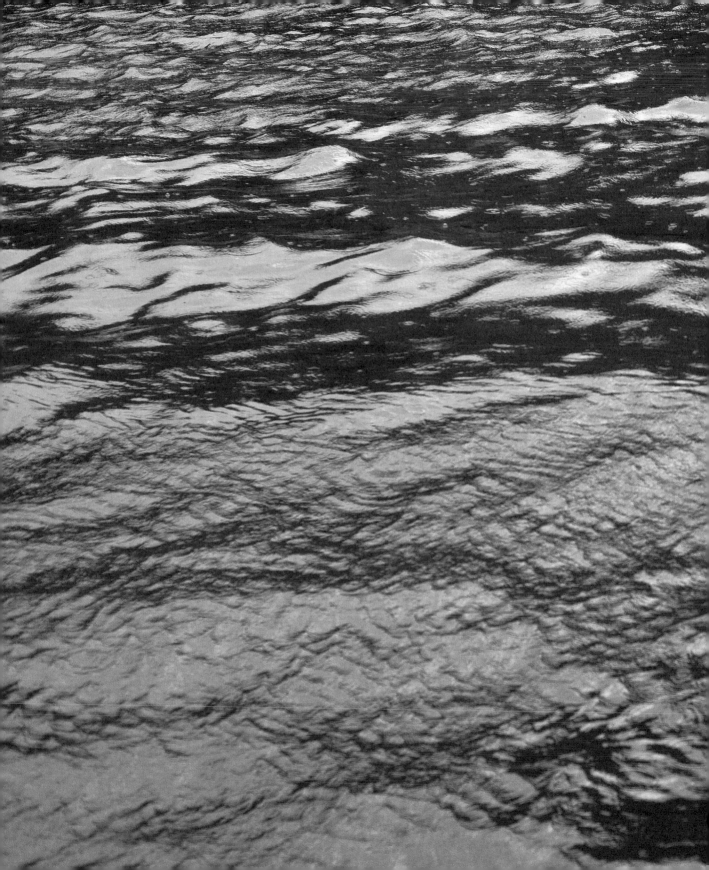

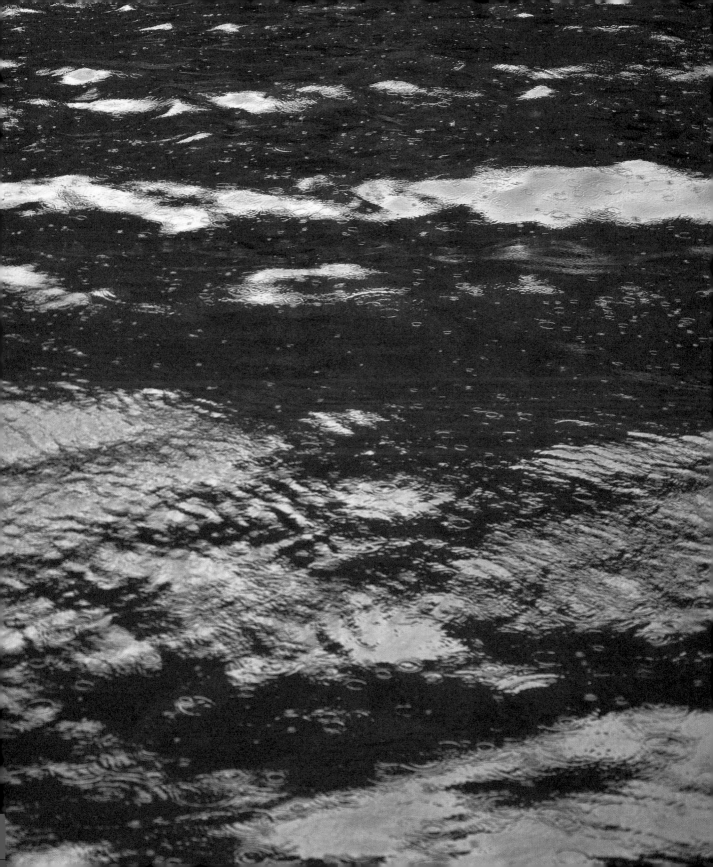

Piazza

VII

CONTORNI

radicchio & roses

❧*Fondi di carciofo*

Artichoke bottoms

8 artichokes
juice of half a lemon
3 tablespoons olive oil
1 garlic clove, chopped
1 tablespoon chopped parsley

These are everywhere. I believe many Venetians buy the frisbee-sized artichoke bottoms ready prepared that I have seen in abundance in the Rialto market. The first outer tough leaves can be thrown away. The next layer of leaves can be saved in a bowl with water & lemon juice. Drain them later & dip the tips in a ramekin of olive oil, lemon, salt & pepper & scrape off with your teeth. The softer inner leaves & all trimmings can go into a vegetable soup or salad.

Use the bigger, wider variety of artichokes if possible. You can make many more of these in your pan — as many as will fill it, depending on their size.

__Cut away the stalk of the artichoke leaving only a couple of centimetres. Now cut that piece off & trim away the outer bitter parts to get to the inner core. (*These can go into a soup.*) The bottoms of the artichokes here need to be flat but the first inner stem bit is good, so save that. Cut away the first couple of centimetres off the top so that it is flat. Now pull away the first tough leaves & discard.

__Next layer the leaves to be saved in a bowl of water with the lemon juice added. The leaves which are still a bit hard but can be eaten in pinzimonio (*raw, dipped in lemon & olive oil*). Then get to the inner bits & trimmings & pop them into the soup pot. If the choke is hairy, cut it away with a small knife or pointed spoon & just have the bottom. If you are not ready to cook them, keep them in lemon water for now.

__Have a pot of broth or water boiling, add the artichoke bottoms and boil gently for 5–10 minutes, or until tender, then lift out with a slotted spoon.

__Heat the oil in a non-stick pan. Add the artichokes & sauté for 2 minutes over high heat to give a nice colour to both sides. Then add the garlic & turn through until you can smell it, season & add the parsley. Cover with a lid & cook for a few moments until the artichokes are tender. Leave the lid on until you serve, with some of the parsley garlic oil dribbled over.

Serves 4–8

Radicchio al limone

Radicchio in lemon

3–4 small or 2 large radicchio
  di Treviso
5 tablespoons olive oil
juice of 1 large lemon

Nice. Bitter. Easy. This is great when radicchio is in season & is a lovely side dish with the liver & onions (page 125) or any secondo you think would go well. Apart from being such a gorgeous colour, radicchio is also very good for us. You need the longer Treviso radicchio for this — the round puffy ones are from nearby bustling Chioggia. With any luck all your radicchio will be similar inside — but the ones with a lot of 'anima' (the white stem) will need to be left over the heat a while longer. It's important that they are soft but not collapsing & are nice & crusty from the cooking. When you cut them, leave the leaves attached at the stem — some leaves may fall away but you will serve them intact. For a spicy kick, add some crumbled peperoncino to the pan. You can make radicchio al vino rosso by using 80 ml (2¾ fl oz/⅓ cup) of red wine instead of the lemon juice.

__You will need a large, good-quality non-stick frying pan that has a lid. Halve or quarter the radicchio, depending on the size, so they fit in your pan in a single layer. Trim away any hard outer leaves if necessary but leave the leaves attached to the stem. Wash the base. Pat dry with kitchen paper.
__Heat the oil in your pan, add the radicchio pieces, cut-side down, & sauté over high heat until the bottoms are cooked & golden. Gently turn over & cook for a few moments to get the underside going, then sprinkle with some salt & pepper & pour over the lemon juice.
__Put the lid on, lower the heat to medium & simmer for about 10 minutes until the radicchio is soft but still attached at the stems & there is some pink syrupy sauce in the pan. The base of the radicchio should be crusty here & the leaves should be soft & delicious. Cook for longer & add a little more liquid if necessary. Sprinkle a little more salt (& *some pepper, if you like*) over the top. Best served warm but also good at room temperature.

Serves 4–6

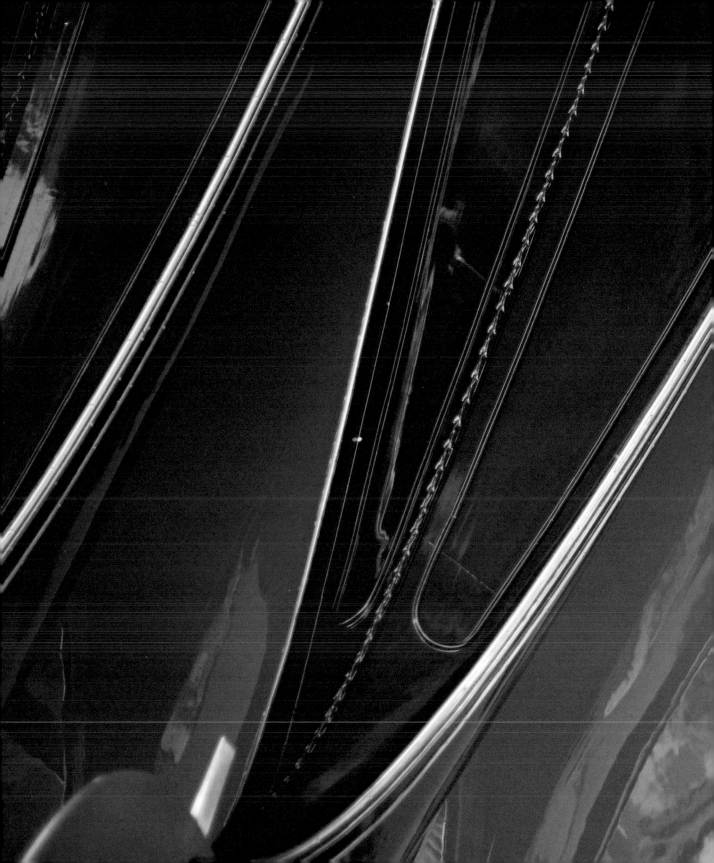

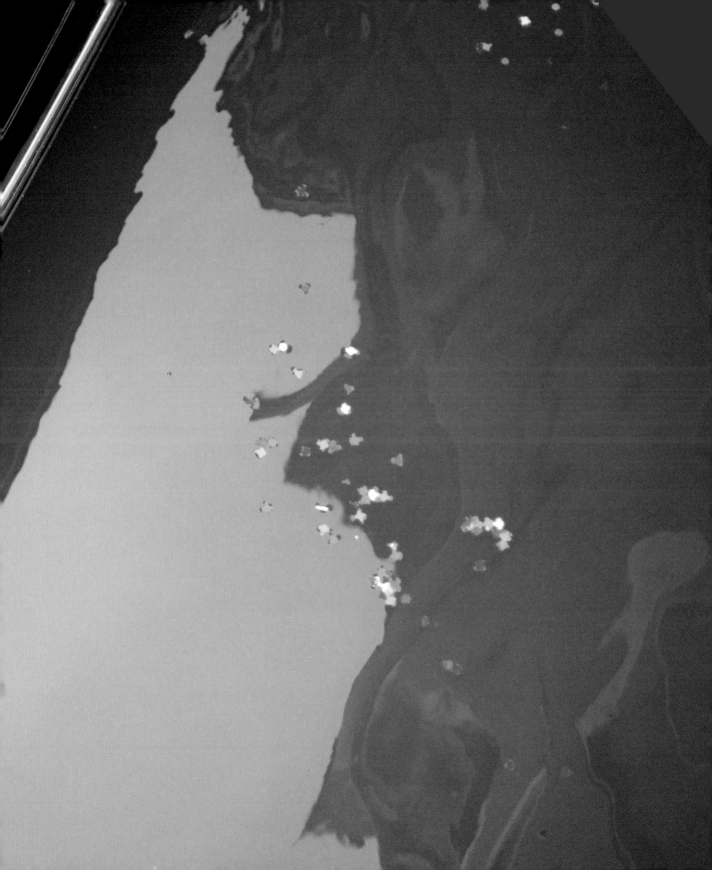

VIII

Tiramisù

3 fresh fresh eggs, preferably
  organic, separated
3 heaped tablespoons sugar
250 g (9 oz) mascarpone
about 125 ml (4 fl oz/½ cup)
  strong coffee
about 3 tablespoons rum, cognac
  or kirsch
about 30 pavesini or small
  savoiardi biscuits
unsweetened cocoa powder,
  for dusting

This can be varied as much as you like: make it less sweet, more sweet; serve it with gratings of dark chocolate on the top; use whatever alcohol you like, such as grand marnier, whisky or marsala. It's also very easy to make double the amount.

My friend Claudia makes this for the children with no alcohol. She mixes milk in with the coffee for a lighter version.

You can either make this in individual dishes or one large one. Small dishes need to be about 5 cm (2 inches) high & long enough across the base to fit the biscuits, so at least 7 cm (2¾ inches). I prefer individual ones but if you'd like to make this in one large dish, it should be about 26 x 18 cm (10 x 7 inches) & 5 cm (2 inches) deep. Mine is slightly wider at the top so I usually have to add more biscuits to the top layer than I do to the bottom.

__Whip the egg whites until very fluffy & white. Next, (*you don't need to wash the beaters*) whip the egg yolks & sugar for an age in a bowl until it is as creamy as you think it will ever get. Mix in the mascarpone & give a quick whisk, then fold in the egg white until lovely, full & *voluminoso*.

__Make your coffee (*if you're using a moka, listen for the beautiful 'ready' sound*). Pour the coffee into a bowl (*if you like, stir in 1 teaspoon of sugar to sweeten it*). Allow to cool a little, then splash in your alcohol.

__Have your 6 dishes ready & dollop a tablespoon of mascarpone into each bowl. Dip a couple of biscuits at a time into the coffee until they have soaked it up, then shake them out well so any excess coffee drips back into the bowl & you don't end up with soggy biscuits. Lay the biscuits over the mascarpone in the bowl. Top with another couple of dollops of mascarpone, then more biscuits, then a final couple of dollops of mascarpone — don't go all the way to the top of your dishes. Put them on a tray in the fridge for at least a couple of hours & dust with cocoa before serving.

Serves 6

Sgroppino

Lemon chill

200 g (7 oz) lemon ice cream
about 4 tablespoons
   chilled prosecco
about 2 tablespoons
   chilled vodka

You can make your own or buy lemon ice cream for this recipe. You can add as much prosecco & vodka as you like here depending how soft your ice cream is & how strong you want this to be. Since I like to serve this after lunch, I've made it fairly mild, bearing in mind that you may have started the meal with prosecco, then moved onto wine & are not looking at passing out for the afternoon. It's much more summery with less alcohol anyway. Many people serve this as a palate cleanser instead of as a dessert. If it's very hot then put your glasses in the freezer for a few minutes before serving.

__Scoop the ice cream into a blender. Splash in the prosecco & vodka & whizz (*the more alcohol you add the more liquidy the mixture will end up*). Pour into glasses & serve at once before it melts completely!

Serves 2

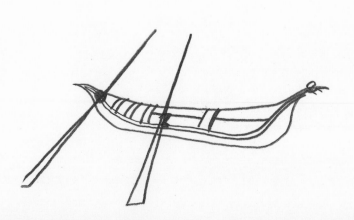

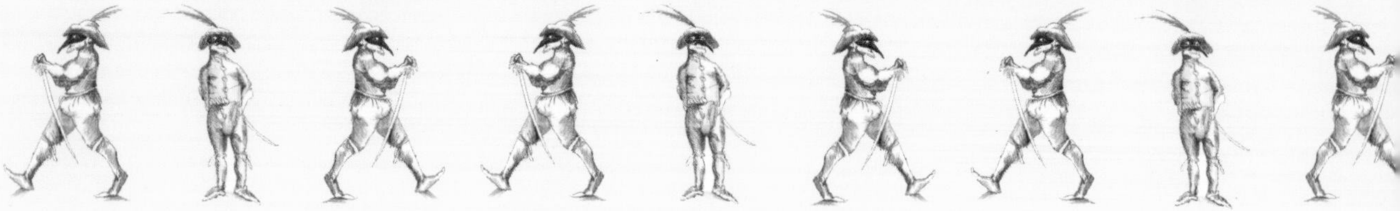

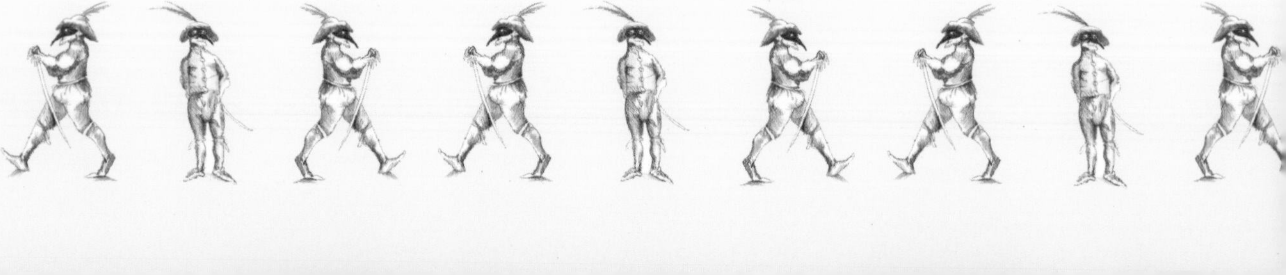

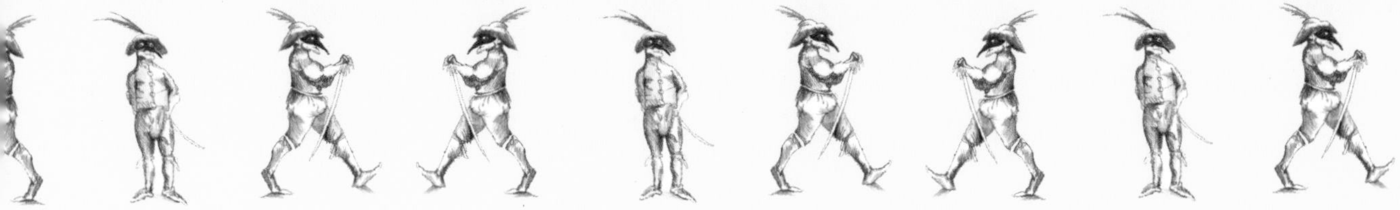

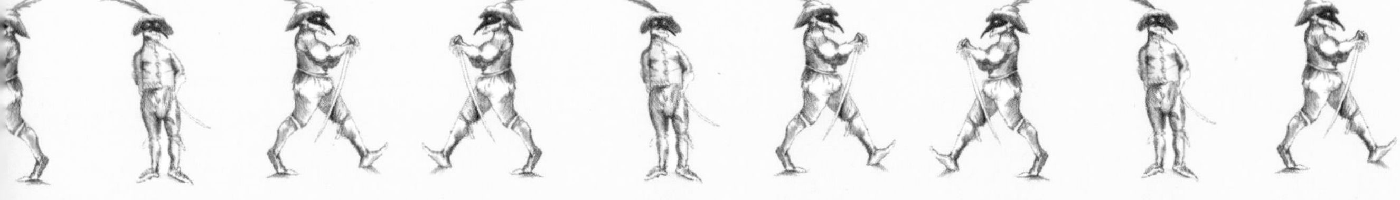

Mare

AB

CD

EF

GHI

JK

LM

NO

PQ

RS

TU

VW

XYZ

AB

CD

EF

GHI

JK

LM

NO

PQ

RS

TU

VW

XYZ

AB

CD

EF

GHI

JK

LM

NO

PQ

RS

TU

VW

XYZ

AB

CD

EF

GHI

JK

LM

NO

PQ

RS

TU

VW

XYZ

PUBLISHED *in* 2009
by MURDOCH BOOKS PTY LTD

MURDOCH BOOKS PTY LIMITED AUSTRALIA
PIER 8/9, 23 HICKSON ROAD,
MILLERS POINT NSW 2000
PHONE: +61 (0)2 8220 2000 FAX: +61 (0)2 8220 2558
www.murdochbooks.com.au

MURDOCH BOOKS UK LIMITED
ERICO HOUSE, 6TH FLOOR, 93–99 UPPER RICHMOND ROAD,
PUTNEY, LONDON SW15 2TG
PHONE: +44 (0)20 8785 5995 FAX: +44 (0)20 8785 5985
www.murdochbooks.co.uk

CHIEF EXECUTIVE
juliet rogers
PUBLISHER
kay scarlett

PHOTOGRAPHY: *manos chatzikonstantis* STYLING & ILLUSTRATIONS: *michail touros* ART DIRECTION & DESIGN: *lisa greenberg*
EDITOR: *daniela bertollo* DESIGNER: *vivien valk and katy wall* FOOD EDITOR: *michelle earl* PRODUCTION: *kita george*

ISBN 9781741966053

Printed in China

Cooking notes:

*You may find cooking times vary depending on the oven you are using. For fan-forced ovens, as a general rule, set the oven temperature
to 20°c (35°f) lower than indicated in the recipe. Important: Those who might be at risk from the effects of salmonella poisoning
(the elderly, pregnant women, young children and those suffering from immune deficiency diseases) should consult their doctor with
any concerns about eating raw eggs.*

AEQVORA TVENS
PORTV·RESIDEO
HIC NECTVNVS